Is College Worth It?
It Depends on
Your Major!

Duard G. Slattery, Jr., BA, MS

Is College Worth It? It Depends on Your Major!

ISBN-13: 978-1539878285

ISBN-10: 1539878287

We have been careful to provide accurate information throughout this book, mostly based on information from the United States Department of Labor, but as in all human endeavors, it is possible that there may be errors or omissions. When making any career decisions, as in any major decision in life, be sure to research many sources, literary, personal, and online.

Credits and Acknowledgments:

The author created this book by drawing upon the work of many other people and organizations. The occupational information is based mostly on data from the United States Department of Labor. The educational taxonomy and classification of academic vs. career majors is from the United States Department of Education. The return on investment (ROI) rankings are based mostly on the data and methods of payscale.com, as acknowledged in detail at the end of this book. Most of the information on health careers comes from explorehealthcareers.org. These organizations are taken to be authoritative sources for this information.

Table of Contents

Introduction

Going to "college"? You might be better off going to the beach.

Going to the beach is free. Going to college is extremely expensive.
And when you are done with four years of liberal arts, you may still be
flippin' burgers and whippin' lattes. If you go to the beach instead, at
least you will be a barista with a tan. And no debt.

It all depends on your major!

Depending on your major, your college education may be useful, or
useless. Your college major may have a very good Return on
Investment, or very poor!

Return on Investment (ROI)

All majors are NOT created equal! Some majors have a very high ROI
(Return on Investment). Some have a very low ROI. Students and
parents need to know which is which!

And there's that little matter of a Trillion dollar debt!

Student debt in America is now at $1.3 trillion. That's trillion with a
"T"! Most student loans (about $1.0 trillion) are backed by the US
government. Some predict that this is the next "bubble" to burst, when
millions of under-employed graduates give up re-paying their debt, and
taxpayers get stuck holding the bill. This is a crisis, both at the
personal and national levels.

Part of the solution is for students and parents to be warned.

So this is it, the book that tells you which majors are useful, *and warns
you which are useless!*

Key to listing for each Major

Key to listing for each Major

See Appendices for full details

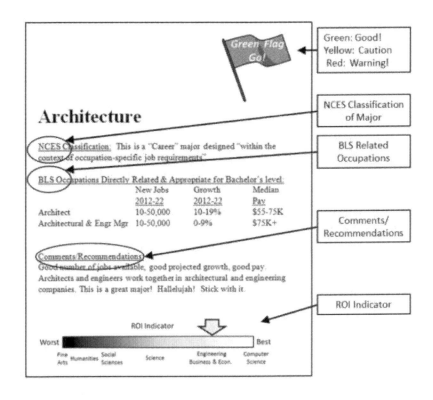

Green: Good!
Yellow: Caution
Red: Warning!

NCES Classification of Major

BLS Related Occupations

Comments/ Recommendations

ROI Indicator

Architecture

NCES Classification. This is a "Career" major designed "within the context of occupation-specific job requirements."

BLS Occupations Directly Related & Appropriate for Bachelor's level.

	New Jobs 2012-22	Growth 2012-22	Median Pay
Architect	10-50,000	10-19%	$55-75K
Architectural & Engr Mgr	10-50,000	0-9%	$75K+

Comments/Recommendations
Good number of jobs available, good projected growth, good pay. Architects and engineers work together in architectural and engineering companies. This is a great major! Hallelujah! Stick with it.

ROI Indicator

Worst ▓▓▓▓▓▓▓▓▓▓▓▓▓▓▓▓▓▓▓▓ Best

Fine Arts / Humanities / Social Sciences / Science / Engineering Business & Econ. / Computer Science

Warning Flag definitions:

Green Flag Go!

Green: Good! There is a good chance of a *bachelor's* degree in this major providing knowledge which leads to a *directly-related* and *well-paying* occupation.

Yellow Flag Caution

Yellow: Caution. There is only a fair chance of a *bachelor's* degree in this major providing knowledge which leads to a *directly-related* and *well-paying* occupation. Many bachelor's graduates in this major will work in un-related fields.

Red Flag Warning!

Red: Warning! There is a poor chance of a *bachelor's* degree in this major providing knowledge which leads to a *directly-related* and *well-paying* occupation. This major is likely to be a dead end for most bachelor's graduates!

Common College Majors
with Warning Flags,
Related Occupations, and
Return on Investment (ROI)

Agriculture (all specialties)

<u>NCES Classification:</u> This is a "Career" major designed "within the context of occupation-specific job requirements". (CIP 01)

<u>BLS Occupations Directly Related & Appropriate for Bachelor's level:</u>

	New Jobs 2012-22	Growth 2012-22	Median Pay
Ag & food scientists	1-5,000	0-9%	$55-75K
Agricultural Engineers	<1000	0-9%	$55-75K

<u>Comments/Recommendations:</u>

Farmers, Ranchers, Farm Mechanics and Technicians all require only a high school diploma or associate's degree. The occupations above require a bachelor's degree. But this field is small, with only a few thousand new jobs projected over 10 years. So this major can only be recommended to those with a family farm, and a guaranteed job. For all others, this looks risky.

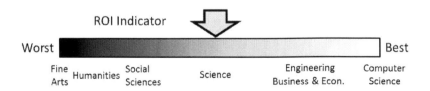

Animal Science

<u>NCES Classification:</u> This is a "Career" major designed "within the context of occupation-specific job requirements". (CIP 01.09)

<u>BLS Occupations Directly Related & Appropriate for Bachelor's level:</u>
None directly related at the bachelor's level.

<u>Comments/Recommendations:</u>
The Animal Scientist and Animal Science teacher jobs typically require a doctoral degree. Animal Breeder and Trainer and Care and Service jobs typically require no formal education. With these occupations requiring a PhD or no degree at all, a bachelor's degree alone is not recommended. The PhD is also risky, as the number of openings is low. A possible bright spot is Animal Trainer, with good openings (5-10,000). While a bachelor's is not necessary for this, animal training can still be a rewarding career for those who love animals.

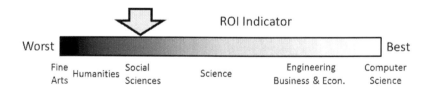

Anthropology

NCES Classification: This is an "Academic" major (a social science) "with minimal regard to specific occupational applications". (CIP 45.02)

BLS Occupations Directly Related & Appropriate for Bachelor's level: None directly related at the bachelor's level.

Comments/Recommendations:
The Anthropologist and Anthropology teaching jobs typically require a master's or doctoral degree. With all the jobs in this field requiring advanced degrees, a bachelor's degree cannot be recommended, unless continuing to the master's or PhD. There are a fair number of openings at the master's level. But in the words of the US Department of Labor, "bachelor's degree holders may find work as assistants or fieldworkers." A bachelor's degree to be an assistant or fieldworker? Wow! You have been warned!

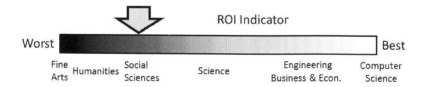

Go to College!

American parents are obsessed with sending their kids to "college", at any cost, and they are backed by the federal government in this obsession. This is a major cause of the college crisis. Parents should research the majors they are paying for, and only pay for majors that have good financial payback! (photo by Christopher Briscoe)

Archeology

NCES Classification: This is an "Academic" major (a social science) "with minimal regard to specific occupational applications". (CIP 45.03)

BLS Occupations Directly Related & Appropriate for Bachelor's level: None directly related at the bachelor's level.

Comments/Recommendations:
The Anthropologist and Archeologist and related teaching jobs typically require a master's or doctoral degree. See the comments for Anthropology. The US Department of Labor lumps together Anthropologist and Archeologist as one "occupation". Again, "bachelor's degree holders may find work as assistants or fieldworkers." You have been warned!

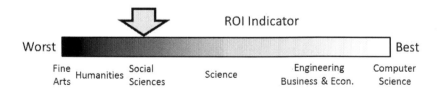

Yellow Flag Caution

Architecture

<u>NCES Classification:</u> This is a "Career" major designed "within the context of occupation-specific job requirements". (CIP 04)

<u>BLS Occupations Directly Related & Appropriate for Bachelor's level:</u>

	New Jobs 2012-22	Growth 2012-22	Median Pay
Architect	5-10,000	0-9%	$75K+
Arch & Engr Mgr	1-5,000	0-9%	$75K+

<u>Comments/Recommendations:</u>
Fair number of jobs available, fair projected growth, good pay. According to the BLS, "Architects will be needed to make plans and designs for…homes, offices, and retail stores" and "demand is projected for architects with a knowledge of green design." But with a high number of students graduating in architecture, "very strong competition… is expected." Those with "up-to-date technical skills (CADD and BIM) will have an advantage." Employment of architects is "strongly tied to the construction industry", so it will be subject to boom-and-bust cycles. Due to competition and risk, yellow flag is warranted.

ROI Indicator

Worst | Best

| Fine Arts | Humanities | Social Sciences | Science | Engineering Business & Econ. | Computer Science |

Architects and engineers build buildings. They get to see their designs literally cast in concrete. They must be creative, knowledgeable, and responsible. And the knowledge they need comes from a bachelor's degree in architecture or engineering, not liberal arts!

Area Studies

(Asian, African, European, Latin American, etc)

<u>NCES Classification:</u> This is an "Academic" major (a social science) "with minimal regard to specific occupational applications". (CIP 05.01)

<u>BLS Occupations Directly Related & Appropriate for Bachelor's level:</u> None directly related at the bachelor's level.

<u>Comments/Recommendations:</u>
The only BLS related occupation, "area, ethnic, and cultural studies teachers, postsecondary" requires a doctoral degree. With the only related occupation requiring a PhD, this major cannot be recommended to anyone, unless you are specifically committing to a doctoral degree and a teaching career. For all others, the ROI is likely to be very low, and most bachelor's grads will probably work in an unrelated field.

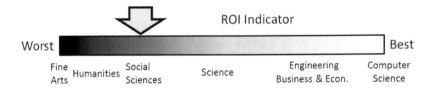

ROI Indicator

Worst   Best

| Fine Arts | Humanities | Social Sciences | Science | Engineering Business & Econ. | Computer Science |

Red Flag Warning!

Art (Fine Arts/Dance/Drama/Film)

<u>NCES Classification:</u> "Academic" major with "minimal regard to specific occupational applications". (CIP 50, except 50.04 and 50.09)

<u>BLS Occupations Directly Related & Appropriate for Bachelor's level:</u>

	New Jobs 2012-22	Growth 2012-22	Median Pay
Art Director	1-5,000	0-9%	$75K+

<u>Comments/Recommendations:</u>
Being a Craft and Fine Artist requires no formal education. Being an Art Teacher (postsecondary) requires a master's degree. Dancers and Actors need no degree. Film Editors don't really need a degree, and there are very few openings. Graphic designers usually need a degree in graphic design. Art director is a possibility, but you have to work your way up to that. The Fine Arts are at the lowest end of the Return on Investment (ROI) scale, according to payscale.com.

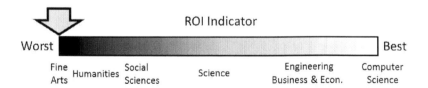

ROI Indicator

Worst — Best

Fine Arts | Humanities | Social Sciences | Science | Engineering Business & Econ. | Computer Science

Art History

NCES Classification: Warning! This is an "Academic" major with "minimal regard to specific occupational applications". (CIP 50.0703)

BLS Occupations Directly Related & Appropriate for Bachelor's level:

	New Jobs 2012-22	Growth 2012-22	Median Pay
Museum technicians	0-1,000	0-9%	$35-55K

Comments/Recommendations:
Museum archivists and curators typically need a master's degree. Museum technicians need a bachelor's, but the number of new jobs is very low! Art History could only be recommended as an interesting major for those students who are already wealthy, and need no job. As this is the study of the Fine Arts, the likely Return on Investment (ROI) for this major is the same as that for the Fine Arts, which is at the very low end.

ROI Indicator

Worst | Best

| Fine Arts | Humanities | Social Sciences | Science | Engineering Business & Econ. | Computer Science |

Astronomy

NCES Classification: Note this is an "Academic" major (a pure science) with "with minimal regard to specific occupational applications". (CIP 40.02)

BLS Occupations Directly Related & Appropriate for Bachelor's level: None for "astronomers" at bachelor's level.

Comments/Recommendations:
The entry-level education for "astronomers" is the PhD. If you are only doing a bachelor's degree, pick another major, or try to parlay astronomy into some other technical field. Some technical jobs may be open to those with science training. Or take a risk and go all the way to the PhD, which is a major commitment, with limited openings.

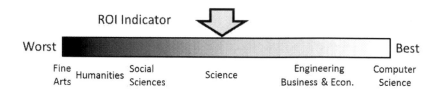

Biochemistry

NCES Classification: This is an "Academic" major (a pure science) with "minimal regard to specific occupational applications". (CIP 26.02)

BLS Occupations Directly Related & Appropriate for Bachelor's level:

	New Jobs 2012-22	Growth 2012-22	Median Pay
Biological technicians	5-10,000	10-19%	$35-55K
Med/clin lab techs	10-50,000	10-19%	$55-75K

Comments/Recommendations:

Positions as a "biochemist" typically require a PhD. The technician and technologist jobs above are appropriate at the bachelor's level. Medical/clinical lab technologist has many openings. Consider changing to bioengineering if you can, for potentially higher pay.

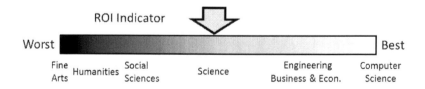

ROI Indicator

Worst | | Best

| Fine Arts | Humanities | Social Sciences | Science | Engineering Business & Econ. | Computer Science |

Bioengineering & Biomedical Engr

NCES Classification: This is a branch of engineering, and is a "Career" major designed "within the context of occupation-specific job requirements". (CIP 14.0501)

BLS Occupations Directly Related & Appropriate for Bachelor's level:

	New Jobs 2012-22	Growth 2012-22	Median Pay
Biological technicians	5-10,000	10-19%	$35-55K
Biomedical engineers	5-10,000	20-29%	$75K+
Med/clin lab technol	10-50,000	10-19%	$55-75K

Comments/Recommendations:
Biomedical engineers have engineering-level pay, and there are also many openings for lab technologists as a backup. This is one of the smaller engineering fields, but outlook is good. Flag is Green!

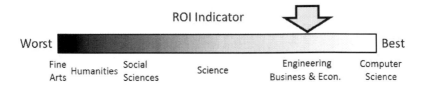

Yellow Flag Caution

Biology

<u>NCES Classification:</u> This is an "Academic" major (a pure science) with "minimal regard to specific occupational applications". (CIP 26)

<u>BLS Occupations Directly Related & Appropriate for Bachelor's level:</u> See Comments/Recommendations below.

<u>Comments/Recommendations:</u>

Under the NCES system for classifying subjects, biology is a huge field! Under biology, the following subjects are included. Each is listed here with a possible corresponding occupation from the BLS occupation listings.

NCES Subject:	Possible related BLS Occupation:
Biochemistry	see listing for this major in this book
Botany	see listing for this major in this book
Cell biology	see Microbiologists
Microbiology	Microbiologists
Zoology	see listing for this major in this book
Genetics	see: Biochemists and biophysicists
Physiology	see: Microbiologists and Zoologists
Pharmacology	see: Medical scientists
Biomathematics	see bioinformatics, biometricians, statisticians
Biotechnology	Many possible applications
Ecology	see: Zoologists and wildlife biologists
Molecular medicine	Molecular biologists, and see: Microbiologists

Neurobiology   possible application to Neurology technicians
Marine biology   Zoologists and wildlife biologists

The occupations listed above may require various levels of education including associate's, bachelor's, master's and PhD degrees.

So it is recommended to biology students that you pick your specialty and research your desired specialty in the BLS Occupational Outlook Handbook. It is not possible to cover all these specialties in the space available in this book.

If you are interested in a more human-oriented "biology" (i.e. health and medicine), check out the health section in this book, and explorehealthcareers.org online, for a huge wealth of data on actual careers and pay and degrees needed.

The ROI indicator is in the middle, for a pure science "biology" major, but it could actually be anywhere along the indicator, depending on your specialty above.

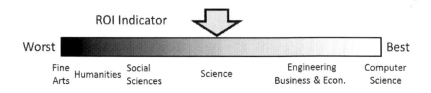

Yellow Flag
Caution

Botany

NCES Classification: This is an "Academic" major (a pure science) with "minimal regard to specific occupational applications". (CIP 26.03)

BLS Occupations Directly Related & Appropriate for Bachelor's level:

	New Jobs 2012-22	Growth 2012-22	Median Pay
Foresters	0 to 999	0-9%	$55-75K
Zoologists -wildlife bio	1-5,000	0-9%	$55-75K

Comments/Recommendations:
The BLS heading for Botanists refers to "Zoologists and wildlife biologists". There are only a few openings for "Foresters". "Forest and conservation technicians" need only an associate's degree or no degree, and openings are low and declining. Change your major, or take a risk and go all the way to the PhD, with limited openings.

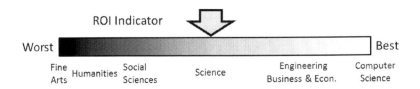

ROI Indicator

Worst | | Best

Fine Arts | Humanities | Social Sciences | Science | Engineering Business & Econ. | Computer Science

Business, Accounting

<u>NCES Classification:</u> This is a "Career" major designed "within the context of occupation-specific job requirements". (CIP 52.03)

<u>BLS Occupations Directly Related & Appropriate for Bachelor's level:</u>

	New Jobs 2012-22	Growth 2012-22	Median Pay
Accountants & auditors	50,000+	10-19%	$55-75K
Budget analysts	1-5,000	0-9%	$55-75K
Financial examiners	1-5,000	0-9%	$75K+
Tax examiners	Declining	Declining	$35-55K

<u>Comments/Recommendations:</u>
Very high jobs available and high projected growth for accountants and auditors. An excellent major with excellent job prospects!

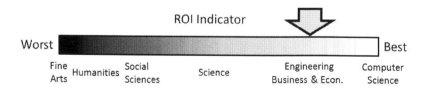

Business, Actuarial Science

NCES Classification: This is a "Career" major designed "within the context of occupation-specific job requirements". (CIP 52.1304)

BLS Occupations Directly Related & Appropriate for Bachelor's level:

	New Jobs 2012-22	Growth 2012-22	Median Pay
Actuaries	5-10,000	20-29%	$75K+

Comments/Recommendations:
Actuaries are essential to the insurance business. Actuaries analyze the financial costs of risk and uncertainty. The bachelor's degree is the typical preparation, plus professional testing and certification. The number of jobs is not as high as that for accountants, but projected *growth* for actuaries is very high. Pay is very good and stated as high as $93,000 in the Occupational Outlook Handbook online. For those willing and able to do analysis, this is an excellent major.

ROI Indicator

Worst | Best

Fine Arts   Humanities   Social Sciences   Science   Engineering Business & Econ.   Computer Science

This grad and his mom are happy because:

1. *He went to community college for the first 2 years, cutting his total college cost almost in half!*
2. *He majored in Business, a practical major with good ROI.*
3. *He arranged an excellent internship, related to both his major and his interests.*
4. *So he already has a great job offer on graduation day!*

Business, Finance

<u>NCES Classification:</u> This is a "Career" major designed "within the context of occupation-specific job requirements". (CIP 52.08)

<u>BLS Occupations Directly Related & Appropriate for Bachelor's level:</u>

	New Jobs 2012-22	Growth 2012-22	Median Pay
Financial analysts	10-50,000	10-19%	$75K+
Financial examiners	1-5,000	0-9%	$75K+
Financial managers	10-50,000	0-9%	$75K+
Personal financial adv	50,000+	20-29%	$55-75K

<u>Comments/Recommendations:</u>
High jobs available, high projected growth, and high pay. It doesn't get much better than this! As a backup to the other occupations, personal financial advisors are projected to be needed in huge numbers. An excellent major with many prospects for employment in various specialties and various businesses.

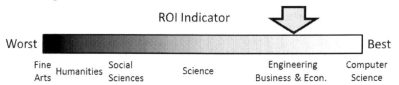

ROI Indicator

Worst | Best

| Fine Arts | Humanities | Social Sciences | Science | Engineering Business & Econ. | Computer Science |

Business, Human Resources

<u>NCES Classification:</u> This is a "Career" major designed "within the context of occupation-specific job requirements". (CIP 52.10)

<u>BLS Occupations Directly Related & Appropriate for Bachelor's level:</u>

	New Jobs 2012-22	Growth 2012-22	Median Pay
Management analysts	50,000+	10-19%	$75K+
Human resource mgrs	10-50,000	10-19%	$75K+
Human res specialists	10-50,000	0-9%	$55-75K

<u>Comments/Recommendations:</u>
High number of jobs, good growth, and good pay for specialists and managers. Go for it, green flag!

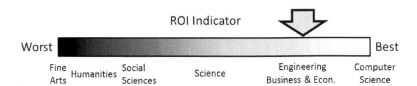

Business, International

NCES Classification: This is a "Career" major designed "within the context of occupation-specific job requirements". (CIP 52.11)

BLS Occupations Directly Related & Appropriate for Bachelor's level: None *directly related* at the *bachelor's level*.

Comments/Recommendations:
Note the yellow flag. In the index of the US Department of Labor Occupational Outlook Handbook, there are no occupations listed under "Business international" or "International business". This business specialty could only be recommended to those with a related family business, and a guaranteed job. For all others, change to another business major, such as finance. Although there are no occupations recognized for this specialty (normally warranting a red flag), the flag is still set at yellow, because those who graduate with this degree will probably be able to parlay their generic business courses into some other business specialty such as finance.

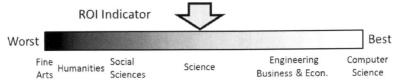

ROI Indicator

Worst   Best

Fine   Humanities   Social   Science   Engineering   Computer
Arts   Sciences   Business & Econ. Science

Business, Management

<u>NCES Classification:</u> This is a "Career" major designed "within the context of occupation-specific job requirements". (CIP 52.02)

<u>BLS Occupations Directly Related & Appropriate for Bachelor's level:</u>

	New Jobs 2012-22	Growth 2012-22	Median Pay
Financial managers	10-50,000	0-9%	$75K+
Management analysts	50,000+	10-19%	$75K+
Admin services mgrs	10-50,000	10-19%	$75K+
Construction mgrs	50,000+	10-19%	$75K+

<u>Comments/Recommendations:</u>
Short answer:
There are many jobs available and good projected growth in various kinds of management and management analysis. Good major, many prospects for employment.

Longer answer:
"Management" is a huge field! Of the hundreds of occupations listed by the US Department of Labor, many, if not all, may have a corresponding kind of manager! It is also important to note that many jobs managing people will require an applicant to have significant experience doing their job first! Some of the kinds of managers recognized by the US Department of Labor are listed below. There is not enough space to cover them all in this book. Pick your specialty

and research any of these more fully in the Occupational Outlook Handbook:

Management analysts
Management consultants, see: Management analysts
Management information systems directors, see: Computer and information systems managers
Management professors, see: Postsecondary teachers
Management scientists, see: Operations research analysts
Managers, see: Funeral service occupations
Managers, see: Public relations and fundraising managers
Managers, see: Administrative services managers
Managers, see: Construction managers
Managers, see: Elementary, middle, and high school principals
Managers, see: Architectural and engineering managers
Managers, see: Food service managers
Managers, see: Lodging managers
Managers, see: Medical and health services managers
Managers, see: Natural sciences managers
Managers, see: Property, real estate, community association managers
Managers, see: Top executives
Managers, see: Purchasing managers, buyers, and purchasing agents
Managing editors, see: Editors

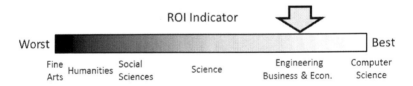

Business, Management Info Systems
(Information Technology, Computing)

NCES Classification: This is a "Career" major designed "within the context of occupation-specific job requirements". (CIP 52.12)

BLS Occupations Directly Related & Appropriate for Bachelor's level:

	New Jobs 2012-22	Growth 2012-22	Median Pay
Comp & info sys mgrs	50,000+	10-19%	$75K+
Comp programmers	10-50,000	0-9%	$55-75K
Comp systems analysts	50,000+	20-29%	$75K+
Info security analysts	10-50,000	30% +	$75K+
Netwk & comp sys adm	10-50,000	10-19%	$55-75K
Software developers	50,000+	20-29%	$75K+
Comp netwk architects	10-50,000	10-19%	$75K+

Comments/Recommendations:
The potential high-paying jobs for this major are too numerous to list on one page! More of the related occupations recognized by the US Department of Labor are listed below. There is not enough space to cover them all in this book. It is left to the reader to research any of this partial list more fully in the Occupational Outlook Handbook:

Business analysts, see: Management analysts

Computer applications developers, see: Software developers
Computer applications engineers, see: Software developers
Computer network architects
Computer operations managers, see: Computer and info sys managers
Computer programmers
Computer security managers, see: Computer and info sys managers
Computer security specialists, see: Information security analysts
Computer systems consultant, see: Computer systems analysts
Computer systems security admins, see: Network and com sys admins
Computer systems security analysts, see: Information security analysts
Computer systems software architects, see: Software developers
Computer systems software engineers, see: Software developers
Database administration manager, see: Database administrators
Database administrators
Data processing managers, see: Computer and info systems managers
Data processing systems analyst, see: Computer systems analysts
Management analysts
Network and computer systems administrators
Network designers, see: Computer network architects
Network developers, see: Computer network architects
Etc.!

Suffice it to say, it doesn't get any better than this! This major shares top honors with Computer science for the highest possible ROI of any bachelor's degrees! See computer science for further occupations that may be open to this major.

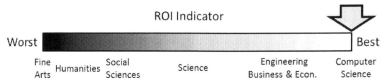

ROI Indicator

Worst | Best

Fine Arts — Humanities — Social Sciences — Science — Engineering Business & Econ. — Computer Science

Majoring in business, and arranging an excellent internship in the junior year, is likely to result in a good job offer coming quicky.

Green Flag Go!

Business, Marketing

NCES Classification: This is a "Career" major designed "within the context of occupation-specific job requirements". (CIP 52.14)

BLS Occupations Directly Related & Appropriate for Bachelor's level:

	New Jobs 2012-22	Growth 2012-22	Median Pay
Market research analys	50,000+	30% +	$55-75K
Sales Reps, General	50,000+	0-9%	$35-55K
Sales Reps, Technical	10-50,000	10-19%	$55-75K

Comments/Recommendations:
Short answer:
There are many jobs available and fair projected growth in various kinds of marketing and sales. There are many prospects for employment.

Longer answer:
The number of jobs open to marketing majors is greatly increased if we include the sales occupations. According to the Wall Street Journal, "marketing and business" are the typical majors that lead to "careers in sales". So both marketing and sales occupations are shown under this major.

It is important to point out that many sales jobs (including two million real estate sales jobs!) require no college degree at all.

In the corporate world, many corporate sales jobs traditionally require a bachelor's degree, either in business or many other generic majors, including liberal arts.

In technical sales, a degree in the appropriate technical field may be required. For example, engineering sales reps typically need a degree in engineering.

Some of the marketing and sales jobs recognized by the US Department of Labor are listed below. It is left to the reader to research any of these more fully in the Occupational Outlook Handbook:

Marketing agents, see: Advertising, promo & marketing managers
Marketing analysts, see: Market research analysts
Marketing consultants, see: Market research analysts
Marketing directors, see: Advertising, promo & marketing managers
Marketing managers, see: Advertising, promo & marketing managers
Sales account managers, see: Sales managers
Sales coordinators, see: Sales managers
Sales directors, see: Sales managers
Sales engineers
Sales executives, see: Sales managers
Sales managers

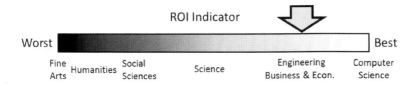

Chemistry

<u>NCES Classification:</u> This is an "Academic" major (a pure science) with "with minimal regard to specific occupational applications". (CIP 40.05)

<u>BLS Occupations Directly Related & Appropriate for Bachelor's level:</u>

	New Jobs 2012-22	Growth 2012-22	Median Pay
Chemists	5-10,000	0-9%	$55-75K

<u>Comments/Recommendations:</u>
One of the more practical of the pure sciences. New jobs are projected to be available, at the bachelor's level, with some growth, and good pay. Chemists have more openings than chemical engineers, but chemical engineers have higher pay. If you are good at chemistry, consider petroleum engineering, with very high growth and high pay.

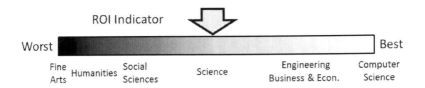

Classics, Classical Languages
(Ancient Latin & Greek language & literature)

NCES Classification: This is an "Academic" major "with minimal regard to specific occupational applications". (CIP 16.12)

BLS Occupations Directly Related & Appropriate for Bachelor's level: None.

Comments/Recommendations:
Between fine arts, philosophy, and the classics, there are no worse majors for finding related employment at the bachelor's level. This cannot be recommended unless you are rich already, because this major has one of the worst possible returns on investment. Parents, tell your kids you are not paying for this!

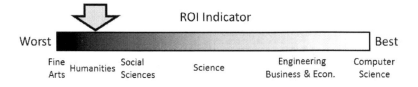

Red Flag Warning!

Communications & Journalism

<u>NCES Classification:</u> This is a "Career" major designed "within the context of occupation-specific job requirements". (CIP 09.01, 09.04)

<u>BLS Occupations Directly Related & Appropriate for Bachelor's level:</u>

	New Jobs 2012-22	Growth 2012-22	Median Pay
Editors	Declining	Declining	$35-55K
Reporters & corresp	Declining	Declining	$35K
Proofreaders	Declining	Declining	$33K
Broadcast news analys	Declining	Declining	$55-75K

<u>Comments/Recommendations:</u>
The print and broadcast media occupations are both declining. The pay is poor, but also irrelevant since there are no new jobs! A Google search yields 10 websites agreeing that communications is one of the worst majors for finding employment. You have been warned.

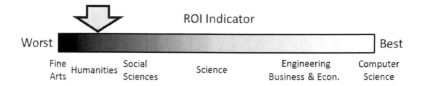

ROI Indicator

Worst   Best

| Fine Arts | Humanities | Social Sciences | Science | Engineering Business & Econ. | Computer Science |

Computer Science

NCES Classification: This is a "Career" major designed "within the context of occupation-specific job requirements". (CIP 11)

BLS Occupations Directly Related & Appropriate for Bachelor's level:

	New Jobs 2012-22	Growth 2012-22	Median Pay
Computer HW engrs	5-10,000	0-9%	$75K+
Computer network arch	10-50,000	10-19%	$75K+
Comp programmer	10-50,000	0-9%	$55-75K
Comp systems analysts	50,000+	20-29%	$75K+
Info security analysts	10-50,000	30% +	$75K+
Netwk & comp sys adm	10-50,000	10-19%	$55-75K
Software developers	50,000+	20-29%	$75K+

Comments/Recommendations:
The potential high-paying jobs for this major are too numerous to list on one page! More of the related occupations recognized by the US Department of Labor are listed below. There is not enough space to cover them all in this book. It is left to the reader to research any of this partial list more fully in the Occupational Outlook Handbook:

Computer applications developers, see: Software developers
Computer applications engineers, see: Software developers
Computer network architects

Computer operations managers, see: Computer and info sys managers
Computer programmers
Computer security managers, see: Computer and info sys managers
Computer security specialists, see: Information security analysts
Computer systems consultant, see: Computer systems analysts
Computer systems security admins, see: Network and com sys admins
Computer systems security analysts, see: Information security analysts
Computer systems software architects, see: Software developers
Computer systems software engineers, see: Software developers
Database administration manager, see: Database administrators
Database administrators
Data processing managers, see: Computer and info systems managers
Data processing systems analyst, see: Computer systems analysts
Management analysts
Network and computer systems administrators
Network designers, see: Computer network architects
Network developers, see: Computer network architects
Etc.!

Suffice it to say, it doesn't get any better than this! According to payscale.com, computer science has the highest possible ROI of any bachelor's degree!

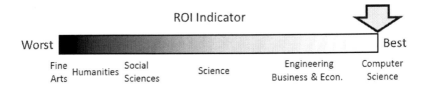

Design & Applied Arts
(Commercial/Graphic Art & Industrial Design)

<u>NCES Classification:</u> This is a "Career" major designed "within the context of occupation-specific job requirements". (CIP 50.04)

<u>BLS Occupations Directly Related & Appropriate for Bachelor's level:</u>

	New Jobs 2012-22	Growth 2012-22	Median Pay
Graphic designers	10-50,000	0-9%	$35-55K
Art Director	1-5,000	0-9%	$75K+
Industrial Designer	1-5,000	0-9%	$55-75K
Fashion designers	Declining	Declining	$55-75K

<u>Comments/Recommendations:</u>
There are many openings for graphic designers, but pay is not so good. Art director and industrial designer are also available at the bachelor's level but with far fewer openings. Fashion design is declining. Caution, yellow flag.

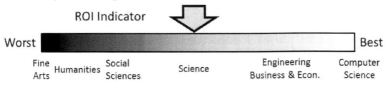

45

Green Flag Go!

Economics

NCES Classification: This is an "Academic" major "with minimal regard to specific occupational applications". (CIP 45.06)

BLS Occupations Directly Related & Appropriate for Bachelor's level:

	New Jobs 2012-22	Growth 2012-22	Median Pay
Market research analys	50,000+	30%+	$55-75K

Etc, see Comments below for many other Business jobs.

Comments/Recommendations:
The entry-level education for "economists" is the PhD. But according to payscale.com, many business jobs are open to those with bachelor's degrees in economics, including the market research work above, with huge openings and huge growth. The extensive ROI data on payscale.com seems to prove that economics majors are taking good-paying business jobs almost as frequently as business majors. Green!

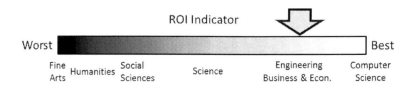

ROI Indicator

Worst | Best

Fine Arts | Humanities | Social Sciences | Science | Engineering Business & Econ. | Computer Science

Education

<u>NCES Classification:</u> This is a "Career" major designed "within the context of occupation-specific job requirements". (CIP 13)

<u>BLS Occupations Directly Related & Appropriate for Bachelor's level:</u>

	New Jobs 2012-22	Growth 2012-22	Median Pay
Kindergarten teachers	10-50,000	10-19%	$35-55K
Elem school teachers	50,000+	10-19% $	35-55K
Secondary school tchrs	50,000+	0-9%	$55-75K
Special ed tchrs, kinder	10-50,000	0-9%	$35-55K
Spec ed tchrs, second	5-10,000	0-9%	$55-75K

<u>Comments/Recommendations:</u>
Very high demand for elementary school teachers, but famously low pay. Also very high demand for secondary (high school) teachers, and much better pay. If you love teaching, then teach.

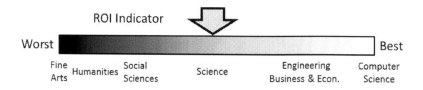

Engineering, Aerospace

NCES Classification: This is a "Career" major designed "within te context of occupation-specific job requirements". (CIP 14.02)

BLS Occupations Directly Related & Appropriate for Bachelor's level:

	New Jobs 2012-22	Growth 2012-22	Median Pay
Aerospace engineers	5-10,000	0-9%	$75K+

Comments/Recommendations:
Growth is a little slow, but pay is very good. According to the US Department of Labor, "employment of aerospace engineers is projected to grow 7 percent from 2012 to 2022", which is slower than average. Aerospace engineering may also be subject to boom and bust cycles, depending on the current outlook at major aerospace employers. So pay is good, but aerospace may be one of the riskier specialties in engineering, like petroleum engineering, so the yellow flag is raised.

ROI Indicator

Worst ▬▬▬▬▬▬▬▬▬▬▬▬▬▬▬▬▬ Best

| Fine Arts | Humanities | Social Sciences | Science | Engineering Business & Econ. | Computer Science |

Engineering, Chemical

<u>NCES Classification:</u> This is a "Career" major designed "within the context of occupation-specific job requirements". (CIP 14.07)

<u>BLS Occupations Directly Related & Appropriate for Bachelor's level:</u>

	New Jobs 2012-22	Growth 2012-22	Median Pay
Chemical Engineers	1-5,000	0-9%	$75K+
Chemists	5-10,000	0-9%	$55-75K
Petroleum Engineers	5-10,000	20-29%	$75K+

<u>Comments/Recommendations:</u>
Chemical engineering, by itself, is a very small field, but well paid.
When the petroleum industry is doing well, chemical engineers should
shoot for jobs in petroleum engineering. But as of 2016, oil prices are
down, so production of new oil and gas is down, so hiring is down.
This field is subject to the boom and bust cycles of the petroleum
industry. So the yellow flag is now raised.

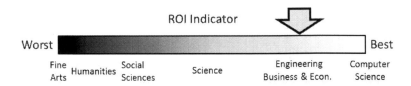

Engineering, Civil

NCES Classification: This is a "Career" major designed "within the context of occupation-specific job requirements". (CIP 14.08)

BLS Occupations Directly Related & Appropriate for Bachelor's level:

	New Jobs 2012-22	Growth 2012-22	Median Pay
Civil Engineers	50,000+	20-29%	$75K+

Comments/Recommendations:
One of the traditional pillars of engineering, which in turn is one of the pillars of society. Very high number of jobs, very high growth, and excellent pay! This is an excellent major, with excellent job prospects. So this is definitely worth some hard work and difficult classes. Stick with it!

ROI Indicator

Worst | | Best

| Fine Arts | Humanities | Social Sciences | Science | Engineering Business & Econ. | Computer Science |

Engineers are really cool, creative, knowledgeable, hard-working, and successful people who make everything from airplanes to zippers. Without engineers, society would literally crumble!

Engineering, Computer Hardware

NCES Classification: This is a "Career" major designed "within the context of occupation-specific job requirements", including both computer hardware and software engineering. (CIP 14.0902)

BLS Occupations Directly Related & Appropriate for Bachelor's level:

	New Jobs 2012-22	Growth 2012-22	Median Pay
Computer HW Engrs	5-10,000	0-9%	$75K+

Comments/Recommendations:
A smaller field than computer software engineering, but still a very good engineering specialty, with very good job prospects, especially in areas like Silicon Valley. If you are into hardware, go for it!

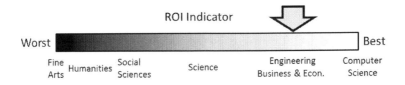

Engineering, Computer Software

NCES Classification: This is a "Career" major designed "within the context of occupation-specific job requirements", including both computer hardware and software engineering. (CIP 14.0903)

BLS Occupations Directly Related & Appropriate for Bachelor's level:

	New Jobs 2012-22	Growth 2012-22	Median Pay
Software dev, apps	50,000+	20-29%	$75K+
Software dev, systems	50,000+	20-29%	$75K+

Comments/Recommendations:
It doesn't get any better than this! This major shares top honors with computer science for the highest possible ROI of any bachelor's degrees! See computer science for further occupations that may be open to this major. This is worth some hard classes! Stick with it!

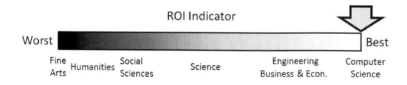

Green Flag
Go!

Engineering, Electrical

<u>NCES Classification:</u> This is a "Career" major designed "within the context of occupation-specific job requirements". (CIP 14.10)

<u>BLS Occupations Directly Related & Appropriate for Bachelor's level:</u>

	New Jobs 2012-22	Growth 2012-22	Median Pay
Electrical Engineers	5-10,000	0-9%	$75K+

<u>Comments/Recommendations:</u>
One of the traditional pillars of engineering, which in turn is one of the pillars of society. Electrical engineers design and develop everything electrical, from smart phones to power plants. An excellent major, to prepare you with detailed and specific knowledge for an excellent career.

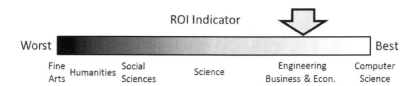

ROI Indicator

Worst | Best

Fine Arts | Humanities | Social Sciences | Science | Engineering Business & Econ. | Computer Science

Green Flag
Go!

Engineering, Environmental

NCES Classification: This is a "Career" major designed "within the context of occupation-specific job requirements". (CIP 14.14)

BLS Occupations Directly Related & Appropriate for Bachelor's level:

	New Jobs 2012-22	Growth 2012-22	Median Pay
Environmental engrs	5-10,000	10-19%	$75K+

Comments/Recommendations:
According to the US Department of Labor, environmental *scientists* use their knowledge of the natural sciences to protect the environment. And environmental *engineers* use the natural sciences and engineering to protect the environment. This is a large and growing field, and good for the earth! This major is "green" in more ways than one!

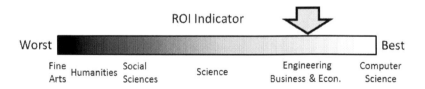

ROI Indicator

Worst | | Best

Fine Arts Humanities Social Sciences Science Engineering Business & Econ. Computer Science

Green Flag Go!

Engineering, Industrial

<u>NCES Classification:</u> This is a "Career" major designed "within the context of occupation-specific job requirements". (CIP 14.35)

<u>BLS Occupations Directly Related & Appropriate for Bachelor's level:</u>

	New Jobs 2012-22	Growth 2012-22	Median Pay
Industrial Engineers	10-50,000	0-9%	$75K+

<u>Comments/Recommendations:</u>
According to the US Department of Labor, industrial engineers "devise efficient ways to use workers, machines, materials, information, and energy to make a product or provide a service." Industrial engineers figure out how to make everything, and how to provide services efficiently too. An excellent major, to prepare you for a large field important to society.

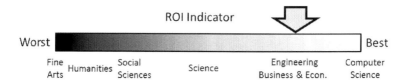

ROI Indicator

Worst | Best

| Fine Arts | Humanities | Social Sciences | Science | Engineering Business & Econ. | Computer Science |

Engineers make everything from A to Z, including airplanes, bicycles, cars, and amphibious off-road vehicles, as seen here.

Green Flag
Go!

Engineering, Mechanical

NCES Classification: This is a "Career" major designed "within the context of occupation-specific job requirements". (CIP 14.19)

BLS Occupations Directly Related & Appropriate for Bachelor's level:

	New Jobs 2012-22	Growth 2012-22	Median Pay
Mechanical Engineers	10-50,000	0-9%	$75K+

Comments/Recommendations:
One of the traditional pillars of engineering, which in turn is one of the pillars of society. Mechanical engineers design and develop everything mechanical, from airplanes to zippers. An excellent major, to prepare you with detailed and specific knowledge to enter a large and important field.

ROI Indicator

Worst | Best

Fine Arts | Humanities | Social Sciences | Science | Engineering Business & Econ. | Computer Science

58

Engineering, Nuclear

<u>NCES Classification:</u> This is a "Career" major designed "within the context of occupation-specific job requirements". (CIP 14.23)

<u>BLS Occupations Directly Related & Appropriate for Bachelor's level:</u>

	New Jobs 2012-22	Growth 2012-22	Median Pay
Nuclear Engineers	1-5,000	0-9%	$75K+

<u>Comments/Recommendations:</u>
There are many complicated factors involved in estimating the outlook for nuclear engineers. According to BLS, nuclear engineers may be needed for US power plant upgrades, foreign upgrades, new developments in nuclear medicine, and for replacements of aging engineers. But on the down side, the public is afraid of nuclear power plants, new petroleum fuels are cheaply available as of this writing, and the number of jobs is small. So the yellow flag is appropriate.

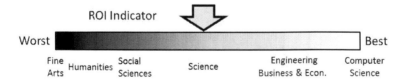

Yellow Flag Caution

Engineering, Petroleum

<u>NCES Classification:</u> This is a "Career" major designed "within the context of occupation-specific job requirements". (CIP 14.25)

<u>BLS Occupations Directly Related & Appropriate for Bachelor's level:</u>

	New Jobs 2012-22	Growth 2012-22	Median Pay
Petroleum Engineers	5-10,000	20-29%	$75K+

<u>Comments/Recommendations:</u>
Petroleum engineering is projected to have high growth, and high pay, as of 2012. But as of 2016, oil prices are down, so production of new oil and gas is down, so hiring is down. This field is subject to boom and bust cycles. So the yellow flag is warranted.

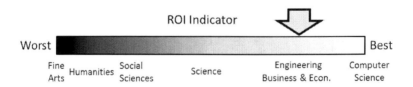

ROI Indicator

Worst   Best

| Fine Arts | Humanities | Social Sciences | Science | Engineering Business & Econ. | Computer Science |

English

NCES Classification: Warning! This is an "Academic" major "with minimal regard to specific occupational applications"! (CIP 23)

BLS Occupations Directly Related & Appropriate for Bachelor's level:

	New Jobs 2012-22	Growth 2012-22	Median Pay
Editors	Declining	Declining	$35-55K
Proofreaders	Declining	Declining	$33K
Writers and authors	1-5,000	0-9%	$55-75K

Comments/Recommendations:

Colleges will say that English prepares you for everything. After all, every job requires speaking, reading and writing English, right? But very few jobs require 4 years of extra English after high school English! Just the handful above, and most those are declining. This is not good. Red flag warning.

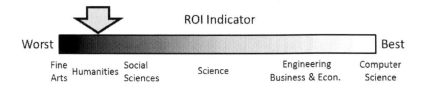

Environmental Science

<u>NCES Classification:</u> This is a "Career" major designed "within the context of occupation-specific job requirements". (CIP 03.0104)

<u>BLS Occupations Directly Related & Appropriate for Bachelor's level:</u>

	New Jobs 2012-22	Growth 2012-22	Median Pay
Environ scientists	10-50,000	10-19%	$55-75K

<u>Comments/Recommendations:</u>
According to the US Department of Labor, environmental *scientists* use their knowledge of the natural sciences to protect the environment. Environmental *engineers* must have a bachelor's degree in engineering. Environmental science is a large and growing field, and good for the earth! This major is "green" in more ways than one!

ROI Indicator

Worst | | Best

Fine Arts | Humanities | Social Sciences | Science | Engineering Business & Econ. | Computer Science

Ethnic Studies

<u>NCES Classification:</u> Warning! This is an "Academic" major "with minimal regard to specific occupational applications"! (CIP 05.02)

<u>BLS Occupations Directly Related & Appropriate for Bachelor's level:</u>
None directly related at the bachelor's level.

<u>Comments/Recommendations:</u>
There are no related occupations at the bachelor's level. According to ethnicstudies.berkeley.edu, "popular options" for graduates in this major include teaching, counseling, and law, all of which require further education! If you want to pay off your student loans after the BA, this is not the way to do it! You will have to change fields to make a living. No person should major in this and stop at the bachelor's level, unless that person is already wealthy, and needs no job.

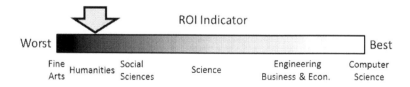

ROI Indicator

Worst | Best

Fine Arts   Humanities   Social Sciences   Science   Engineering Business & Econ.   Computer Science

All over America, people are saving up for "college". Why? Some majors will have a good return on investment, but some will have a terrible return. Before deciding to invest in college at all, we should do some serious research into the product we are purchasing!

Food & Nutrition

NCES Classification: This is a "Career" major designed "within the context of occupation-specific job requirements". (CIP 19.05)

BLS Occupations Directly Related & Appropriate for Bachelor's level:

	New Jobs 2012-22	Growth 2012-22	Median Pay
Dietitians & nutrition	10-50,000	20-29%	$55-75K
Agric & food scientist	1-5,000	0-9%	$55-75K

Comments/Recommendations:
According to BLS Occupational Outlook Handbook, "most dietitians and nutritionists have a bachelor's degree and have participated in supervised training through an internship or as part of their coursework. Many states require dietitians and nutritionists to be licensed." High number of new jobs, high growth, and good pay. Go for it!

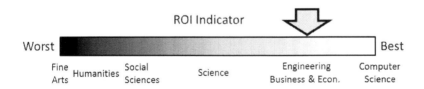

Geography

<u>NCES Classification:</u> Warning! This is an "Academic" major "with minimal regard to specific occupational applications"! (CIP 45.0701)

<u>BLS Occupations Directly Related & Appropriate for Bachelor's level:</u>

	New Jobs 2012-22	Growth 2012-22	Median Pay
Geographers	0-1,000	20-29%	$55-75K

<u>Comments/Recommendations:</u>
Geography has such a tiny number of projected openings, this major cannot be recommended. Many grads will probably have to change fields to make a living.

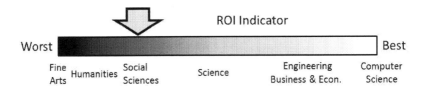

Green Flag
Go!

Geology & Geosciences

<u>NCES Classification:</u> This is an "Academic" major "with minimal regard to specific occupational applications"! (CIP 40.06)

<u>BLS Occupations Directly Related & Appropriate for Bachelor's level:</u>

	New Jobs 2012-22	Growth 2012-22	Median Pay
Geoscientists	5-10,000	10-19%	$75K+

<u>Comments/Recommendations:</u>
In the BLS data, the geologist and geophysicist occupations both refer to the "geoscientist" occupation. According to the BLS Occupational Outlook Handbook, "the need for energy, environmental protection, and responsible land and resource management is projected to spur demand for geoscientists in the future." With good growth and high pay, this academic science major is rated green, like an engineering major!

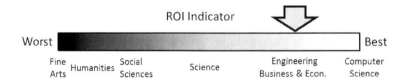

ROI Indicator

Worst   Best

Fine Arts   Humanities   Social Sciences   Science   Engineering Business & Econ.   Computer Science

Health, General Services & Sciences

Special Note regarding Health Services & Sciences:

The field of Health Services & Sciences is gigantic, and far beyond the space limitations of this book. The reader is strongly urged to refer to explorehealthcareers.org to research health careers. This site has a huge wealth of information on over 100 health careers, and corresponding training needed.

Note that the appropriate training for health careers may or may not require a college degree at all! The appropriate training needed for health careers may include high school, associate's, bachelor's, master's, PhD, MD, and many certificates and licenses! Again, see explorehealthcareers.org for details.

If you are interested in health majors and health careers, be sure to research health career training before you spend $100k on college!

NCES Classification:
Partial List of NCES College Subjects in Health:

51) HEALTH PROFESSIONS AND RELATED PROGRAMS.
51.00) Health Services/Allied Health/Health Sciences, General.
51.01) Chiropractic.
51.02) Communication Disorders Sciences and Services.

51.04) Dentistry.

51.06) Dental Support Services and Allied Professions.

51.07) Health and Medical Administrative Services.

51.08) Allied Health and Medical Assisting Services.

51.09) Allied Health Diagnostic, Intervention, and Treatment

51.10) Clinical/Medical Laboratory Science/Research and Allied

51.11) Health/Medical Preparatory Programs.

51.12) Medicine.

51.14) Medical Clinical Sciences/Graduate Medical Studies.

51.15) Mental and Social Health Services and Allied Professions.

51.17) Optometry.

51.18) Ophthalmic & Optometric Support Services & Allied

51.19) Osteopathic Medicine/Osteopathy.

51.20) Pharmacy, Pharmaceutical Sciences, and Administration.

51.21) Podiatric Medicine/Podiatry.

51.22) Public Health.

51.23) Rehabilitation and Therapeutic Professions.

51.24) Veterinary Medicine.

51.25) Veterinary Biomedical and Clinical Sciences.

51.27) Medical Illustration and Informatics.

51.31) Dietetics and Clinical Nutrition Services.

51.32) Bioethics/Medical Ethics.

51.33) Alternative and Complementary Medicine and Medical Systems.

51.34) Alternative and Complementary Medical Support Services.

51.35) Somatic Bodywork and Related Therapeutic Services.

51.36) Movement and Mind-Body Therapies and Education.

51.37) Energy and Biologically Based Therapies.

51.38) Registered Nursing, Nursing Admin, Research and Clinical

51.39) Practical Nursing, Vocational Nursing and Nursing Assistants.

BLS Related Occupations:
Partial List of BLS Occupations in Health and Medicine:
(Some may be appropriate for bachelor's degree, and some may need lower or higher degrees.)

Health, safety, and environmental managers, see: Health and safety engineers
Health actuaries, see: Actuaries
Health and safety inspectors, occupational, see: Occupational health and safety specialists
Healthcare administrators, see: Medical and health services managers
Healthcare documentation specialists, see: Medical transcriptionists
Healthcare executives, see: Medical and health services managers
Healthcare manager, see: Medical and health services managers
Health education specialists, see: Health educators and community health workers
Health educators and community health workers
Health information coders, see: Medical records and health information technicians
Health information managers, see: Medical and health services managers
Health psychologists, see: Psychologists
Health records technicians, see: Medical records and health information technicians
Health sciences librarians, see: Librarians
Health services directors, see: Medical and health services managers
Health services managers, see: Medical and health services managers
Medical and health services managers
Medical appliance technicians, see: Dental and ophthalmic laboratory technicians and medical appliance technicians
Medical assistant instructors, see: Career/technical education teachers
Medical assistants
Medical coders, see: Medical records and health information technicians
Medical directors, see: Medical and health services managers
Medical engineers, see: Biomedical engineers

Medical epidemiologist, see: Epidemiologists
Medical equipment technicians, see: Medical equipment repairers
Medical equipment technologists, see: Medical equipment repairers
Medical health researchers, see: Medical scientists
Medical laboratory technicians, see: Medical and clinical lab technologists and technicians
Medical laboratory technologists, see: Medical and clinical lab technologists and technicians
Medical records administrators, see: Medical & health services mgrs
Medical records and health information technicians
Medical records specialists, see: Medical records and health inf techs
Medical record transcribers, see: Medical transcriptionists
Medical research scientists, see: Medical scientists
Medical scientists
Medical services managers, see: Medical and health services managers
Medical social workers, see: Social workers

Comments/Recommendations:
1. Research health careers in explorehealthcareers.org.
2. Note that you may not need college at all, for many excellent health occupations!
3. Health careers are awesome, and make the world a better place every day!

The flag is green because there are tons of good jobs here!

The ROI may vary, depending on the specialty chosen.

Nurses and health careers are awesome. They make the world a better place every day. But be sure to get appropriate training! Many of these careers, including nursing, do not require a 4-year college degree! Check out explorehealthcareers.org before you spend $100k on college!

Health, Registered Nursing

<u>NCES Classification:</u> This is a "Career" major designed "within the context of occupation-specific job requirements". (CIP 51.38)

<u>BLS Occupations Directly Related & Appropriate for Bachelor's level:</u>

	New Jobs 2012-22	Growth 2012-22	Median Pay
Registered nurses	50,000+	10-19%	$55-75K

<u>Comments/Recommendations:</u>
Nursing has a huge number of projected new jobs available, good growth, good pay, and you get to make the world a better place every day! It must be noted however that registered nurse training can be done in either a 4-year program, or a 2-year program. With the jobs, growth, and pay above, the ROI will be even better if you can do this in a 2-year program! Be sure to check out explorehealthcareers.org!

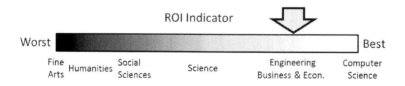

ROI Indicator

Worst | Best

Fine Arts | Humanities | Social Sciences | Science | Engineering Business & Econ. | Computer Science

Red Flag Warning!

History

NCES Classification: This is an "Academic" major "with minimal regard to specific occupational applications"! (CIP 54)

BLS Occupations Directly Related & Appropriate for Bachelor's level:

	New Jobs 2012-22	Growth 2012-22	Median Pay
Museum technicians	0-1,000	0-9%	$35-55K

Comments/Recommendations:
According to US Department of Labor data, "historians" typically need a master's degree, and history professors typically need a PhD, and there are only a few openings for museum technicians. So this major cannot be recommended to anyone stopping at the bachelor's level. And continuing on to the more advanced degrees is risky, with few projected openings. For use as a pre-law major, see the comments in the Legal Studies and Philosophy sections in this book. At the *bachelor's* level, red flag is warranted.

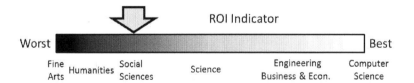

ROI Indicator

Worst — Best

Fine Arts | Humanities | Social Sciences | Science | Engineering Business & Econ. | Computer Science

Yellow Flag Caution

Hospitality Admin/Mgt
(Includes Tourism, Hotel/Motel/Resort Mgt)

NCES Classification: This is a "Career" major designed "within the context of occupation-specific job requirements". (CIP 52.09)

BLS Occupations Directly Related & Appropriate for Bachelor's level:

	New Jobs 2012-22	Growth 2012-22	Median Pay
Lodging managers	0-1,000	0-9%	$35-55K

Comments/Recommendations:
The hotel, motel, and lodging manager occupations at small hotels can be done with a high school diploma. But most large, full-service hotels do require a bachelor's degree to apply for hotel manager. Very low number of new jobs, and pay is not so good. Be careful, yellow flag.

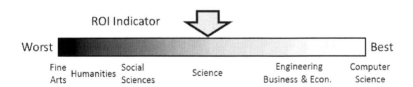
ROI Indicator

Worst — Best

Fine Arts | Humanities | Social Sciences | Science | Engineering Business & Econ. | Computer Science

Choosing your major poorly presents many risks, including the risk of moving back home, going back to your old high school job, and facing both while carrying the weight of a $31K loan. Struggling like that is one way to "grow up", but it's so unnecessary, and you could do so much better! Take a gap year to work, take time to research better majors, and research health and other non-college careers!

Languages, Foreign, All

<u>NCES Classification:</u> Warning! This is an "Academic" major "with minimal regard to specific occupational applications"! (CIP 16)

<u>BLS Occupations Directly Related & Appropriate for Bachelor's level:</u>

	New Jobs 2012-22	Growth 2012-22	Median Pay
Interpreter & translator	10-50,000	30%+	$35-55K

<u>Comments/Recommendations:</u>

There is a large number of openings and very high projected growth for interpreters and translators. But note very carefully that there is a huge difference between having a BA in a foreign language and being a professional translator!

According to the US Department of Labor, the most important requirement for this job is not the bachelor's degree, but rather to have "native-level fluency in English and at least one other language". Also, it makes a huge difference which language you choose. One of the largest employers in this field is the Federal Bureau of Investigation, and the FBI is looking for the "critical" languages, including Arabic, Chinese, Farsi, Korean, Punjabi, Russian, Spanish, Urdu, and Vietnamese. This is a far cry from the traditional French taught at so many colleges!

So to get employment as a translator, you should have native-level fluency in one of the critical languages, and fluency in English. So a BA in French is not going to cut it! For all the non-critical languages, the flag should be red! But having a BA in one of the critical languages might help, so the flag is yellow.

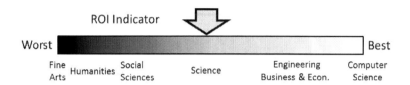

Red Flag Warning!

Legal Studies

<u>NCES Classification:</u> This is a "Career" major designed "within the context of occupation-specific job requirements". (CIP 22)

<u>BLS Occupations Directly Related & Appropriate for Bachelor's level:</u>
None are directly related at the bachelor's level

<u>Comments/Recommendations:</u>
This major is not recommended for paralegals, because paralegals only need an associate's degree. And as a pre-law major, it is beyond the scope of this book, as this book is about occupations appropriate at the bachelor's level. So what can you do with a *bachelor's* degree in legal studies?
A search of college web sites yields many claims that a bachelor's degree in legal studies will "help you to pursue" many jobs. But with a little further research, these claims do not hold up well, as seen in the table below.
So usefulness *at the bachelor's level, at the level of a 4-year college degree*, is poor. So the red flag is raised.

Jobs proposed by colleges for a bachelor's degree in Legal Studies	Findings in US Dept of Labor Bureau of Labor Statistics (BLS) data
Paralegal, Legal Asst	Only associate's needed
Social Worker	See Sociology in this book
Court Administrator	Not listed in BLS
FBI Agent	FBI is mostly seeking "hard sciences", and "critical languages"
Investigator	BLS refers to Claims Adjuster, needing only HS
Immigration Inspector	Not listed in BLS
Contract Administrator	BLS refers to Purchasing Manager, typically needing any generic BA plus experience as Purch Agt.

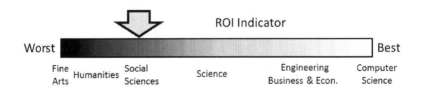

Liberal Arts & Sciences
(Includes Gen Studies & Humanities)

<u>NCES Classification:</u> Warning! This is an "Academic" major "with minimal regard to specific occupational applications"! (CIP 24.01)

<u>BLS Occupations Directly Related & Appropriate for Bachelor's level:</u> None directly related at bachelor's level.

<u>Comments/Recommendations:</u>
Payscale.com data show that humanities majors have very low Return on Investment (ROI). This major could only be recommended to those who are already wealthy and need no job, or to those who plan to teach in these subjects. Colleges say liberal arts majors learn valuable lessons in "critical thinking" and "teamwork" that are important in the workplace. But if your purpose is to learn generic workplace skills, then you should go to work immediately, instead of college, and learn workplace skills while you are *earning* $30k per year, instead of *spending* $30k per year!

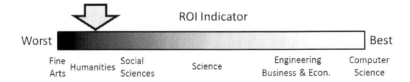

If your major is liberal arts,

"Now what?" indeed!

Library Science

NCES Classification: This is a "Career" major designed "within the context of occupation-specific job requirements". (CIP 25)

BLS Occupations Directly Related & Appropriate for Bachelor's level: None directly related at bachelor's level.

Comments/Recommendations:
According to the BLS, librarians typically need a master's degree, while library *technicians* and *assistants* need only an associate's degree or high school diploma. So with a bachelor's degree, you would be either under-educated or over-educated! So stopping at the bachelor's level cannot be recommended to anyone. There is a large number of openings for librarians, so most people in this major should probably continue to the master's. But with no directly related occupations at the bachelor's level, the red warning flag must be raised.

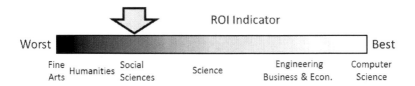

Materials Science

<u>NCES Classification:</u> Warning! This is an "Academic" major "with minimal regard to specific occupational applications"! (CIP 40.10)

<u>BLS Occupations Directly Related & Appropriate for Bachelor's level:</u>

	New Jobs 2012-22	Growth 2012-22	Median Pay
Materials engineers	0-1,000	0-9%	$75K+
Materials scientists	0-1,000	0-9%	$75K+

<u>Comments/Recommendations:</u>
Very small number of openings, but high pay. If you are in this major and want to stick with it, be sure to start your job search early, and arrange a good internship if you can. Consider other engineering and chemistry-related occupations in this book that have a higher number of new jobs available.

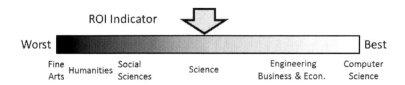

Green Flag
Go!

Mathematics

NCES Classification: This is an "Academic" major "with minimal regard to specific occupational applications" (CIP 27), but read on…

BLS Occupations Directly Related & Appropriate for Bachelor's level:

	New Jobs 2012-22	Growth 2012-22	Median Pay
Mathematicians	0-1,000	20-29%	$75K+
Software dev, apps	50,000+	20-29%	$75K+
Software dev, systems	50,000+	20-29%	$75K+
Actuaries	5-10,000	20-29%	$75K+
Financial analysts	10-50,000	10-19%	$75K+
Comp programmers	10-50,000	0-9%	$55-75K

Comments/Recommendations:

Many math grads work in analytical jobs in insurance, engineering, software, finance, and biotech. So these occupations are added to the list above. The result is math grads have very good job prospects! Green!

ROI Indicator

Worst   Best

| Fine Arts | Humanities | Social Sciences | Science | Engineering Business & Econ. | Computer Science |

Music

NCES Classification: Warning! This is an "Academic" major "with minimal regard to specific occupational applications"! (CIP 50.09)

BLS Occupations Directly Related & Appropriate for Bachelor's level:

	New Jobs 2012-22	Growth 2012-22	Median Pay
Music director & comp	1-5,000	0-9%	$35-55K
Producer & director	1-5,000	0-9%	$55-75K

Comments/Recommendations:

If music is your passion, then go for it, but be ready for anything. The "music directors and composers" listed by the US Department of Labor are those formal "conductors" who "lead orchestras" and work in "religious organizations" and "concert halls".

In reference to more popular music, in the dry bureaucratic language of the US Department of Labor, "there are no formal educational requirements for those interested in writing [or performing] popular music." Well, that's for sure! Katy Perry for example lived in L.A for 5 years "with no money, writing bad checks, and selling my clothes to make rent", according to Seventeen magazine.

Of course we hear many stories of musical performers going from "rags to riches", but we don't hear about the thousands who remain in rags.

As for producers and directors, BLS says "most producers and directors have a bachelor's degree and several years of work experience in an occupation related to motion picture, TV, or theater production, such as an actor, film and video editor, or cinematographer." So a bachelor's degree alone is certainly not enough for that occupation. Most producers and directors have to work their way up!

Again, if music is your passion, go for it, but be ready for anything, be ready to go anywhere, and be ready to live in motels, or even in your car. Low number of jobs, low growth, and very risky getting paid at all. This is one of the performing arts, at the worst end of the ROI scale, according to payscale.com. Red flag.

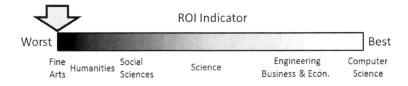

Yellow Flag
Caution

Natural Resources & Conservation
(Includes Fishing, Forestry, Wildlife)

NCES Classification: This is a "Career" major designed "within the context of occupation-specific job requirements". (CIP 03)

BLS Occupations Directly Related & Appropriate for Bachelor's level:

	New Jobs 2012-22	Growth 2012-22	Median Pay
Conservation scientists	0-1,000	0-9%	$55-75K

Comments/Recommendations:
Such a small number of new openings! What's going on? BLS says "employment of conservation scientists and foresters is projected to grow 3 percent from 2012 to 2022, slower than the average for all occupations. Heightened demand for American timber and wood pellets will help increase the overall job prospects for conservation scientists and foresters." Not many jobs, not much growth, yellow flag.

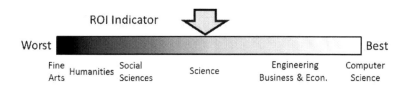

Oceanography,
Chemical/Physical

<u>NCES Classification:</u> This is an "Academic" major "with minimal regard to specific occupational applications"! (CIP 40.0607)

<u>BLS Occupations Directly Related & Appropriate for Bachelor's level:</u>

	New Jobs 2012-22	Growth 2012-22	Median Pay
All Geoscientists	5-10,000	10-19%	$75K+

<u>Comments/Recommendations:</u>

Note the NCES classifications for "oceanography" split this field into three academic areas:
1. CIP 40.0607, Oceanography, Chemical and Physical, under Geosciences and Physical Sciences
2. CIP 26.1302, Marine Biology and Biological Oceanography, under Ecology, and Biology
3. CIP 29.0306, Operational Oceanography, under Military Technologies

This section covers only the first area above, Oceanography, Chemical and Physical. The second area, Marine Biology, is covered in this book under Biology. The third area has no related occupations in the BLS data, and is not covered in this book.

In the BLS data, the title "oceanographer" is referred to geoscientist, and geoscientist is defined to include oceanographers, seismologists, geologists and other specialties. While the openings and growth and pay are all good for geoscientists, it is not clear from the BLS data if the outlook for oceanographers is the same as that for the much larger group of geoscientists as a whole. Without separate BLS data for oceanographers, this is hard to determine.

Scripps Institution website yields a few more data points: "Although the demand for new positions in oceanography is small, scientists are needed to replace the present teachers and researchers." "The average yearly salary for an oceanographer with a bachelor's degree (in 2009) was $33,254. Postdoctoral researchers average salary ranged from $37,400 to $49,452. Academic salaries for assistant professors ranged from $53,200 to $80,300 while tenured professors can make between $100,000 to $150,000. The average yearly government salary (in 2009) for oceanographers [typically with advanced degree] was $105,671." (Source: https://scripps.ucsd.edu/education/careers)

Suggestion: Arrange an internship, or a summer job, or even a volunteer position with Scripps Institution of Oceanography or Woods Hole Oceanographic Institution . If you cannot do that, this looks risky. Do further research if you are serious about oceanography.

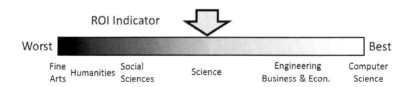

Red Flag Warning!

Philosophy

<u>NCES Classification:</u> Warning! This is an "Academic" major "with minimal regard to specific occupational applications"! (CIP 38.01)

<u>BLS Occupations Directly Related & Appropriate for Bachelor's level:</u> None. There is no such occupation as "philosopher"!

<u>Comments/Recommendations:</u>
For those who stop at the bachelor's level, this is amazingly impractical. All grads with only a bachelor's in philosophy will need to do something else to make a living. But it is interesting to note that philosophy works fine as a pre-law major. (Philosophy majors do very well on the Law School Admissions Test, LSAT). But this book is about related occupations at the bachelor's level, and there ain't none! If you love philosophy, then read about it on the side. You will need to do something else to make a living, maybe carpenter, maybe lawyer.

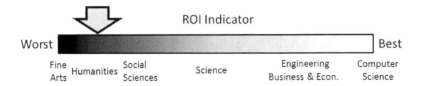

ROI Indicator

Worst — Best

Fine Arts | Humanities | Social Sciences | Science | Engineering Business & Econ. | Computer Science

91

Physics

NCES Classification: This is an "Academic" major (a pure science) "with minimal regard to specific occupational applications" (CIP 40.08).
But read on...

BLS Occupations Directly Related & Appropriate for Bachelor's level:

	New Jobs 2012-22	Growth 2012-22	Median Pay
Software dev, apps	50,000+	20-29%	$75K+
Software dev, systems	50,000+	20-29%	$75K+
Comp programmers	10-50,000	0-9%	$55-75K
Nuclear Engineers	1-5,000	0-9%	$75K+
Petroleum Engineers	5-10,000	20-29%	$75K+

Comments/Recommendations:

The occupation "physicist" typically requires a PhD. But the physics major, at the bachelor's level, like mathematics, is widely applicable in engineering and computer programming.

According to payscale.com, physics is among the top ten majors that pay you back the best at the bachelor's level. It is ranked between computer science and mechanical engineering. Physics is the king of all sciences, but more importantly for this book, it is also widely applicable at the bachelor's level! Green flag!

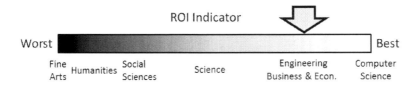

Red Flag Warning!

Political Science

<u>NCES Classification:</u> This is an "Academic" major (social science) "with minimal regard to specific occupational applications". (CIP 45.10)

<u>BLS Occupations Directly Related & Appropriate for Bachelor's level:</u> None directly related at the bachelor's level.

<u>Comments/Recommendations:</u>
According to the US Department of Labor, "Political scientists need a master's degree or Ph.D. in political science". Also political science is very often used as a pre-law degree, but again, that requires more advanced degrees.

So what can you do with a *bachelor's* degree in political science? A search of college web sites yields many jobs that "you can do" with a bachelor's degree in political science. But with a little further research, most of these suggested jobs are not directly related, or not at the right level, as seen in the table below.

So usefulness *at the bachelor's level*, at the level of a 4-year college degree, is poor. So the red flag must be raised.

Jobs proposed by college websites for a bachelor's degree in Political Science	Findings in US Dept of Labor Bureau of Labor Statistics (BLS) data
Campaign Worker	Job title not in US Dept of Labor BLS. Many are volunteers.
City Manager	AKA General Manager, refers to Top Exec in BLS. Typically need master's & many years exp
Business Administrator	Too vague. See specific business jobs, and needed degrees, in this book.
Executive Search Consultant	Assuming personnel recruiter. Bachelor's in Business HR preferred.
Executive Assistant	BLS refers this to "secretaries". Really, after 4 years of college??
Financial Planner	BS in Business or Finance preferred.
Paralegal, Legal Asst	Only associate's degree needed
Political Correspondent	Usually have bachelor's degree in journalism or communications
Political Consultant	Need master's or PhD
Urban Policy Planner	Usually need master's degree

ROI Indicator

Worst ▮▮▮▮▮▮▮▮▮▮▮ Best

Fine Arts   Humanities   Social Sciences   Science   Engineering Business & Econ.   Computer Science

Red Flag Warning!

Psychology

<u>NCES Classification:</u> Warning! This is an "Academic" major (in the Social Sciences) with "minimal regard to specific occupational applications". (CIP 42)

<u>BLS Occupations Directly Related & Appropriate for Bachelor's level:</u>

	New Jobs 2012-22	Growth 2012-22	Median Pay
Social Worker	5-10,000	0-9%	$35-55

<u>Comments/Recommendations:</u>
There are way too many psychology majors. There are projected to be only 5-10,000 new jobs available in a closely related occupation over the 10-year period from 2012 to 2022, or less than 1,000 per year. But there are over 90,000 new bachelor's degrees in psychology per year! So for over 90% of psychology graduates with just a bachelor's degree, psychology will be a dead end. Most will need to find work in some other field.

Indeed, actual data shows that bachelor's graduates in psychology take many different jobs including nanny, equipment operator, counselor, office clerk, research assistant, teacher, military officer, lab coordinator, cost estimator, ranch hand, taxi driver, animal trainer, and even engineer (after returning to school for another degree, in engineering).

Academic websites suggest that psychology provides skill sets that are valuable to employers, including critical thinking, problem solving, project management, and interpersonal and team work skills. But if the goal is to learn generic workplace skills, you could have worked for four years and been *paid* to learn workplace skills, instead of *paying*!

See the table in the political science section above. Much of that discussion applies here also.

Many anecdotes are available online, such as this one:
"Both me and my girlfriend got our BA in psychology in 2012. After nearly a year of attempting to find jobs we both had to settle for clerk positions because that was the most pay we could find. $12/hr. Every job out there for psych won't list the pay on the application because they all offer peanuts." [sic]
(Source: http://psychology.about.com/od/psychology101/fl/Are-There-Too-Many-Psychology-Majors.htm)

This is sad.

So a bachelor's degree in psychology cannot be recommended, except as a path for a few (only about 7%) toward the PhD. Students and parents, the red flag is raised, you have been warned.

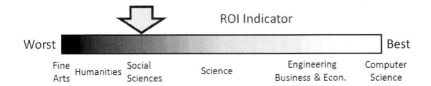

Public Administration

NCES Classification: This is a "Career" major designed "within the context of occupation-specific job requirements". (CIP 44.04)

BLS Occupations Directly Related & Appropriate for Bachelor's level:

	New Jobs 2012-22	Growth 2012-22	Median Pay
Social/community serv	10-50,000	20-29%	$55-75K

Comments/Recommendations:
According to the US Department of Labor, "social and community service managers coordinate and supervise social service programs and community organizations." They work for "nonprofit organizations, private for-profit social service companies, and government agencies." Strong growth will be driven by "increases in the elderly population", and other factors. Some experience and/or master's may also be required. Large field, strong growth, and good pay. Green flag.

ROI Indicator

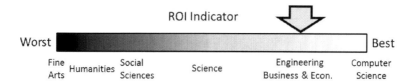

Worst						Best
Fine Arts	Humanities	Social Sciences	Science	Engineering Business & Econ.	Computer Science	

Yellow Flag
Caution

Public Relations & Advertising

NCES Classification: This is a "Career" major designed "within the context of occupation-specific job requirements". (CIP 09.09)

BLS Occupations Directly Related & Appropriate for Bachelor's level:

	New Jobs 2012-22	Growth 2012-22	Median Pay
Public relations spec	10-50,000	10-19%	$35-55K
Public relations mgrs	5-10,000	10-19%	$75K+
Advertising sales agts	Declining	Declining	$35-55K
Advert/promo mgrs.	1-5,000	0-9%	$75K+

Comments/Recommendations:
Public relations has a good number of projected openings, but only fair growth, fair pay, and strong competition. Advertising is declining slightly, especially in newspapers but this will be "offset by increases in internet and television advertising sales", according to the BLS. Mixed signals, caution, yellow flag.

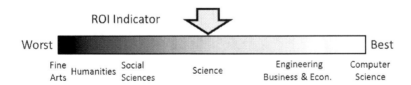

ROI Indicator

Worst | | Best

Fine Arts   Humanities   Social Sciences   Science   Engineering Business & Econ.   Computer Science

*To avoid this scenario on graduation day, you must do some serious
research in advance, to learn the difference between those majors that
are useful, and those that are useless! It also helps a lot to arrange an
excellent internship in the junior year!*

Religious Studies

NCES Classification: This is an "Academic" major "with minimal regard to specific occupational applications". (CIP 38.02)

BLS Occupations Directly Related & Appropriate for Bachelor's level:

	New Jobs 2012-22	Growth 2012-22	Median Pay
Clergy	10-50,000	10-19%	$35-55K
(Priest, Minister, Pastor, etc)			

Comments/Recommendations:

According to O*Net, 67% of the clergy (Priest, Minister, Pastor, etc) have a master's degree , and 24% have a bachelor's. Religious studies professors need a PhD. In the NCES classification of academic subjects, religious studies is closely related to philosophy. So most the comments already stated for philosophy also apply here, including the tendency for many grads to go to law school. Most of the clergy have a master's, so most of the jobs above will not be open at the bachelor's level. Therefore the yellow flag is appropriate at bachelor's level.

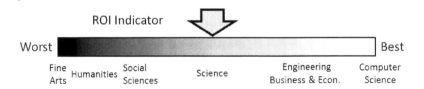

Red Flag Warning!

Sociology

<u>NCES Classification:</u> Warning! This is an "Academic" major (in the Social Sciences) "with minimal regard to specific occupational applications"! (CIP 45.11)

<u>BLS Occupations Directly Related & Appropriate for Bachelor's level:</u>

	New Jobs 2012-22	Growth 2012-22	Median Pay
Social Worker	5-10,000	0-9%	$35-55

<u>Comments/Recommendations:</u>

There are way too many sociology majors. There are projected to be only 5-10,000 new jobs available in a closely related occupation over the 10-year period from 2012 to 2022, in other words only about 1,000 per year. But there are about 30,000 new bachelor's degrees in sociology per year! So for over 90% of sociology graduates with just a bachelor's degree, sociology will be a dead end. Most will need to find work in some other field.

Indeed, actual data shows that graduates with bachelor's degrees in sociology take many jobs including waitress, salesperson, office worker, police officer, research assistant, baseball coach, military officer, retail clerk, operations planner, program assistant, social worker, communications technician, health counselor, etc.
(Sources: Virginia Tech website, UCSD website)

So it could be said that sociology prepares you for everything, but it could also be said that it prepares you for nothing. It does not provide you with any closely related specific knowledge for any specific occupation, except for the single related occupation listed above.

College web sites suggest that social sciences provide skill sets that are valuable to employers, including critical thinking, problem solving, project management, and interpersonal and team work skills. But if the goal is to learn generic workplace skills, you could have worked for four years and been *paid* to learn workplace skills, instead of *paying*!

Sociology is included in the "8 College Degrees with the Worst Return on Investment", according to salary.com.

So a bachelor's degree in sociology is definitely not recommended, except as a path for very few toward the PhD. Students and parents, the red flag is raised, you have been warned.

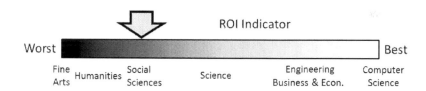

Statistics

<u>NCES Classification:</u> This is an "Academic" major "with minimal regard to specific occupational applications". (CIP 27.05)

<u>BLS Occupations Directly Related & Appropriate for Bachelor's level:</u>

	New Jobs 2012-22	Growth 2012-22	Median Pay
Statisticians	5-10,000	20-29%	$75K+
Actuaries	5-10,000	20-29%	$75K+
Market research analys	50,000+	30% +	$55-75K

<u>Comments/Recommendations:</u>

Some excellent comments regarding job opportunities for statistics majors at the bachelor's level come from the University of Toronto:

"With an undergraduate degree in Statistics...In a management or sales position in an insurance company, you will be able to understand actuarial data…. In a marketing or market research setting, lots of the data come from sample surveys and are subjected to standard statistical analyses."

According to the BLS, "statisticians typically need a graduate degree in statistics or mathematics. However, there are an increasing number of positions available for those with only a bachelor's degree." This is great news for those at the bachelor's level!

In addition, statistics should have good transferability to actuaries, and to market research analysts, especially the latter, which is very large and growing very fast. With this transferability, especially to the huge field of marketing analysis, the green flag is raised!

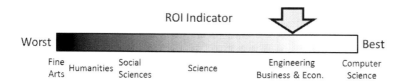

Urban Studies

NCES Classification: This is an "Academic" major (social science) "with minimal regard to specific occupational applications". (CIP 45.12)

BLS Occupations Directly Related & Appropriate for Bachelor's level:

	New Jobs 2012-22	Growth 2012-22	Median Pay
Urban/region planners	1-5,000	10-19%	$55-75K

Comments/Recommendations:
According to the US Department of Labor, "Urban and regional planners *usually* need a master's degree". So this occupation is listed above, at the bachelor's level, even though it will not *usually* be available at the bachelor's level. This is not much to go on, when there are only 1-5,000 new jobs projected anyway!

So what else can you do with a *bachelor's* degree in urban studies? A search of college web sites yields many jobs that you can "pursue". But with a little further research, these claims do not hold up well, as seen in the table below.

Low number of openings (very low after accounting for the master's holders taking most!). Warning, red flag.

Jobs proposed by college websites for a bachelor's degree in Urban Studies	Findings in US Dept of Labor Bureau of Labor Statistics (BLS) data
Urban Policy Planner	Usually need master's degree
City Manager	AKA General Manager, refers to Top Exec in BLS. Typically need master's and many years experience.
Lawyer	Requires a law degree
Lobbyist	BLS refers this to Public Relations Specialist. Better to major in Public Relations. See section in this book.
Professor	Requires a PhD
Public Administrator	See Public Administration section in this book
Public Policy Director	BLS refers to political scientist, need a master's degree or Ph.D
Zoning Administrator	BLS only includes zoning engineers, under engineering

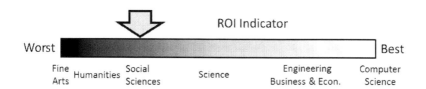

Yellow Flag
Caution

Zoology

<u>NCES Classification:</u> This is an "Academic" major (a pure science) "with minimal regard to specific occupational applications". (CIP 26.07)

<u>BLS Occupations Directly Related & Appropriate for Bachelor's level:</u>

	New Jobs 2012-22	Growth 2012-22	Median Pay
Zoologists	1-5,000	0-9%	$55-75K

<u>Comments/Recommendations:</u>
It is possible to work at the bachelor's level as a zoologist. But with few new jobs, and low growth, it is not likely. See the larger section in this book on biology. If you can, change majors to another field under biology. If it is too late to change majors, then you may need to try to parlay biology courses taken into some other job under biology.

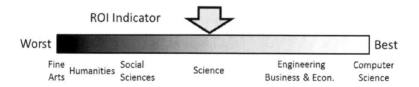

ROI Indicator

Worst   Best

Fine Arts   Humanities   Social Sciences   Science   Engineering Business & Econ.   Computer Science

Conclusions

There are at least two serious problems with "college" in America:

- At the individual level, millions of students and parents are making poor investments in college majors, investments that are "not worth it", in liberal arts and humanities and social sciences.
- At the national level, we all have a looming economic crisis in the form of $1.3 trillion in student debt, much of it owed by graduates who have learned no specific job skills in college.

Based on the research for this book, it is possible to recommend actions for many of us to take:

In High School:

- High school students should plan for careers and for life, not just plan to get into college.
- High school students should read this book, or one like it, and research potential careers in the US Department of Labor Occupational Outlook Handbook.
- High schools should require students to research potential careers.
- Before going to college, all students should have at least some idea what they want to do with their life and career, in order to have any idea what they need to get out of their time in college!

In College:

- Consider community college! All the 4-year degrees in this book will have TWICE the return on investment, if you can cut the cost in half! According to collegeboard.org, average annual 4-year college costs are $9,410, $23,890, and $32,410, for in-state, out-of-state, and private college respectively. But public 2-year colleges average just $3,440 per year! So four years at a 4-year college may well cost $100,000. Instead, take the first two years at a 2-year college, and your total cost might be about $57,000 which is almost a reduction by half!

- College students should arrange internships related to their major as soon as possible, at least by the junior year. If your major is applicable to a professional field, this is the way to get started. If your major is *not* applicable to a professional field, you need to know that, as soon as possible!
- College parents should research majors and only pay for majors that have good chances of financial payback!
- College students should be planning for careers and for life, not just planning how to finish college.
- College students should read this book, or one like it, and research potential careers using the US Department of Labor Occupational Outlook Handbook.
- Colleges should require students to research potential careers.
- Except for those few students who are wealthy and need no job, and those who are committing to a PhD, and those who are at elite colleges, a *bachelor's* degree (and only a *bachelor's* degree) is not recommended for anybody, in the following subjects:
    - Liberal Arts (fine arts, performing arts, dance, music, and including Humanities and Social Sciences below)
    - Humanities (all foreign languages, liberal/general studies, philosophy, religious studies)
    - Social Sciences (anthropology, geography, political science, sociology, psychology, area studies, ethnic studies, history)

For all students, after High School and during College:
- This is obvious, but it needs to be stated: Don't start paying $30,000 per year for college, if you have no idea why you are going!
- If you have no plans for life, then you should take time off to work in the real world, until you do! People should figure out what they want to do while they are *making* $30,000 per year, instead of *spending* $30,000 per year! Attending college is a very expensive way to figure out what you want to do!

In Business:

- Businesses should not require applicants to have a generic unspecified "college degree". Do not perpetuate the BA-for-all mentality. For many jobs, it is not necessary to force applicants to go through four years of generic college, in turn forcing many to go into debt. *And, it is harmful to the American economy to do so!*
- Businesses should ask themselves: What is the specific knowledge, skill, personality, or aptitude that you are looking for? And what is the most efficient way to get those traits?
- Basic reading, writing, science and math aptitude can be determined by SAT scores, or other testing. It is not necessary for an applicant to spend $100,000 for four years in college, just to prove aptitude! *Using college merely as an aptitude tester is extremely inefficient, and harmful to the American economy!*
- Don't try to hire forever. Hire for a conditional period, an internship. This will give the lowest-risk proof that a certain person has the knowledge, skill, personality, or ability to learn that you need.

In Government, most important of all:

- The government, just like parents, should only pay for majors that have good financial payback!
- The government should not subsidize generic unspecified bachelor's degrees! Perpetuating the BA-for-all mentality is *harmful to the American economy!*
- The government should not guarantee student loans, without regard to major subject and without regard to a person's likely ability to pay back!
- Why are we subsidizing a generation of philosophy majors to work in coffee shops? We cannot afford that, and we don't want that!

The Last Word

The last word is given to an otherwise unknown student named "Steve" who wrote this email to PBS.org in response to a report on the value of a bachelor's degree in liberal arts:

I'm in my final semester of a Liberal Arts degree in History, and I have learned a lot along the way. Unfortunately for me, no one cares. I have a 3.76 GPA, but most companies would rather hire someone with a 3.0 and a B.S. in business for entry level positions. A degree is only worth as much as those people doing the hiring think it is worth. I would recommend to anyone pursuing a Liberal Arts degree, to change majors immediately.

You have been warned.

Appendices & References

- **Key Terminology**
- **Actual first jobs taken by new bachelor's graduates**
- **References**
- **About the Author**

NCES Classification:

NCES is the National Center for Education Statistics, under the Institute of Education Sciences, within the U.S. Department of Education. The NCES has classifed all college majors as either "academic" or "career" type majors, defined as follows:

Academic majors: "Formal programs of study…typically designed to be comprehensive, *theoretical, and decontextualized (from a labor market perspective)….with minimal regard to specific occupational applications.*
Examples are fine arts, philosophy, pure sciences, social sciences, etc.

Career majors: "Formal programs of study designed to impart knowledge and skills that represent the relevant accumulated *knowledge within the context of occupation-specific job requirements….often explicitly linked to occupational skill demands."*
Examples are agriculture, business, engineering, health, etc.

(Source: "Undergraduate Enrollments in Academic, Career, and Vocational Education", NCES publication 2004–018, Feb 2004, available from NCES website. Emphasis added.)

CIP code:
The NCES has created a detailed "taxonomy" for classifying all college subjects. All subject areas are identified with a CIP code (Classification of Instructional Programs). The CIP code is provided in this book for each major, to indicate clearly and unambiguously what subject matter is covered. See the listing on Oceanography for an excellent example.

BLS Occupations Directly Related & Appropriate for Bachelor's level:

This book is about finding occupations that are both *directly related* to the subject matter learned, and also appropriate at the *bachelor's level*. For example, in the case of legal studies, many college websites propose that a bachelor's degree in legal studies will help you to "pursue" many jobs such as paralegal, social worker, FBI agent, etc. But in this book, many of these suggestions are rejected, because they are either *not directly related*, or *not at the bachelors level*, as shown below:

Jobs proposed by colleges for a bachelor's degree in Legal Studies	Reasons why these suggestions are rejected in this book
Paralegal	Level is wrong. Only an associate's degree is needed.
Social Worker	Not directly related. Sociology is more closely related.
FBI Agent	Not directly related to content FBI is seeking, mostly "hard sciences", and "critical languages".
Investigator	Level is wrong. BLS refers this to Claims Adjuster, needing only high school.

So in the case of legal studies, and many other majors in this book, the finding is "None". That means there are NO *directly related* BLS occupations, *at the bachelor's level*, for many college majors!

<u>Key to BLS data:</u>

The data presented in this section is taken directly from the online Occupational Outlook Handbook, of the Bureau of Labor Statistics (BLS), under the US Department of Labor. This is commonly known as "the BLS data".

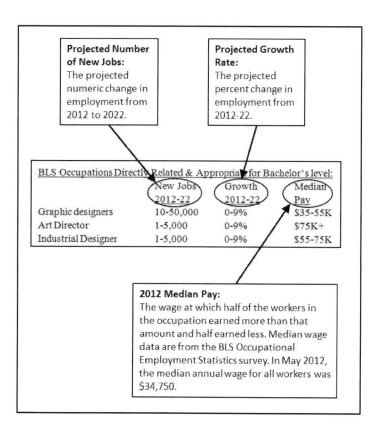

Comments/Recommendations:

These are the comments and recommendation from this author, based
on data from the US Department of Education NCES, data from the
US Department of Labor BLS, data from the other references listed,
and based on additional research, experience, and judgment, of the
author.

Exceptions from the general trends are noted in this section. For
example physics, one of the pure sciences (normally in the middle of
the ROI indicator at yellow) is given a green flag for high applicability
and transferability to engineering. And nuclear engineering, one of the
engineering specialties (normally green) is given a yellow flag for a
variety of complicated factors currently depressing that field.

Note regarding Teaching:
Teaching jobs are not included in the "related occupations" in this
book. Teaching jobs are always assumed to be open to anyone with a
bachelor's in any subject, and a teaching credential. So instead of
adding the teaching jobs to every single major listing, the space is
saved, and the ever-present possibility of being a teacher is not
explicitly listed.

Return on Investment (ROI) Indicator

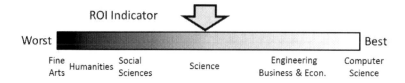

ROI Indicator

Worst   Best

Fine   Humanities   Social   Science   Engineering   Computer
Arts   Sciences   Business & Econ.   Science

This indicator shows relative Return on Investment (ROI) for groups of majors, based mostly on data and methodology from payscale.com.

To develop this ROI indicator, ROI data was taken from payscale.com and first converted into the original bar chart below as follows:

The major with the best ROI (computer science) was assigned the value of 100%, and the other majors are compared to that. For example, engineering has a 20-year return of $0.985M compared to computer science at $1.094M. (Averages were taken of the top 15 schools in all cases.) So the relative ROI of engineering is 0.985/1.094 which is 90%. In this way the original chart below is created here for all major groups listed in payscale.com. And the chart below is the basis for the ROI indicators shown for each major.

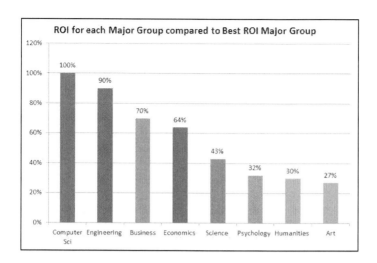

From the bar chart above, the ROI indicator was created, with computer science at the highest (Best) end, and art at the lowest (Worst) end.

<u>Actual First Jobs taken by new bachelor's graduates</u>

On various websites, various colleges say you can do many jobs with a bachelor's degree in history, as shown in the first column below:

Jobs proposed by colleges for a bachelor's degree in History	Actual First Jobs taken by history bachelor's grads in 2014
Historical Org researcher Think Tank researcher Writers and Editors Journalists Records Managers Librarians Information Managers Lawyers Paralegals Litigation Support Legislative Staff Work Historians in Businesses	Community Outreach Worker Digitization Specialist (aka scanner) Assistant Account Executive Restaurant Waiter Media Marketing Associate Campus Intern Clerk Fundraising Lead Entry-level Mgt Trainee Target Sales Floor worker Army Officer ETC. Plus ~20% doing master's Plus ~20% unemployed

The second column shows a listing of actual first jobs taken.
(Source: Virginia Tech website,
http://www.career.vt.edu/postgraduationsurveyreport/postgrad.html)

Kudos to Virginia Tech for clear reporting of actual "first destinations"! All colleges should report this! This is what we really need to know!

References

1. U.S. Department of Labor, Bureau of Labor Statistics (BLS), Occupational Outlook Handbook: http://www.bls.gov/ooh/

2. US Department of Labor, Bureau of Labor Statistics (BLS), Occupational Outlook Handbook , A-Z Index of Occupations: http://www.bls.gov/ooh/a-z-index.htm#

3. US Department of Labor, Bureau of Labor Statistics (BLS), Occupational Outlook Handbook, Occupation Finder: http://www.bls.gov/ooh/occupation-finder.htm

4. US Department of Labor, Bureau of Labor Statistics (BLS), Occupational Employment Statistics: http://www.bls.gov/oes/current/oes_stru.htm

5. U.S. Department of Education, Institute of Education Sciences, National Center for Educational Statistics (NCES): https://nces.ed.gov/

6. US Department of Education, Institute of Education Sciences, National Center for Education Statistics (NCES), Classification of Instructional Programs (CIP) codes: https://nces.ed.gov/ipeds/cipcode/browse.aspx?y=55

7. Payscale.com. College Return On Investment (ROI) data: http://www.payscale.com/college-roi/

8. Bennet, William J. (former U.S. Secretary of Education) and Wilezol, David, "Is College Worth It?", Thomas Nelson, 2013

9. Explorehealthcareers.org, information on health careers: http://explorehealthcareers.org/en/Field/1/Allied_Health_Professions

10. Fastcompany.com, "The 3 Types of People Who May Want To Consider Skipping College", Michael Grothaus: http://www.fastcompany.com/3048024/the-future-of-work/the-3-types-of-people-who-may-want-to-consider-skipping-college?partner=rss

11. Virginia Tech website, www.career.vt.edu/postgraduationsurveyreport/postgrad.html

12. O*NET OnLine, https://www.onetonline.org/
O*Net has vast information, some of it taken from the same BLS sources referenced above, and much of it easier to use than the BLS web pages. O*Net has detailed listings of "related" occupations, but note the listings may include occupations at all levels, including unskilled labor, high school, associate's, bachelor's, and higher degrees.

13. Marketwatch national student loan debt clock, http://www.marketwatch.com/story/every-second-americans-get-buried-under-another-3055-in-student-loan-debt-2015-06-10, this website shows the national student loan debt ticking up in real time, at over $2,700 per second!

About the Author:

Duard Slattery has a BA in psychology from Stanford, and an MS in engineering from San Diego State. After the BA degree, and subsequent jobs as a ranch hand, taxi driver, animal trainer, and cold-calling salesman, Duard returned to college for a degree in engineering, financed by student jobs and student loans. He is now semi-retired from a successful career in engineering and software. He is working on several books and splits his time between homes in San Diego and Tahoe.

The author with wife and daughter at daughter's high school graduation. Off to College!

For additional copies of

**Is College Worth It?
It Depends on
Your Major!**

go to
www.amazon.com

Made in the USA
San Bernardino, CA
14 November 2016